# Pembrokeshire
# Backroads

# Pembrokeshire Backroads

## Six Driving Tours Through History

**Andrea and Ed Sutcliffe**

**Front cover photo**: Near Mynachlog-ddu, in the eastern Preseli Hills

**Back cover photos, clockwise from top:** Carreg Samson, near Trefin; St Govan's Chapel, near Bosherston; Llawhaden Castle; and Lamphey Bishop's Palace

*All photographs and maps by Andrea and Ed Sutcliffe*

## Dolbadau Road Press

Revised June 2017

*Dedicated to the memory of my mother*

Nesta Griffiths Johnson
of
Cilgerran, Pembrokeshire
1921-2008

St Dogmaels
Cilgerran
Strumble Head
Newport
Fishguard
Porthgain
Rosebush
St Davids
Solva
Ramsey
Island
Haverfordwest
Narberth
Skomer
Island
Broad Haven
Milford Haven
Skokholm
Island
Angle
Tenby
Pembroke
Caldey Island
St Govan's

# Pembrokeshire

# Contents

# Introduction

Our goal for this book is to help visitors and residents alike explore the scenic beauty of Pembrokeshire as well as learn a little about its deep and rich past.

Pembrokeshire is widely known as a wonderful place for walking, and books on the topic are plentiful. We are devoted Pembrokeshire Coast Path walkers ourselves. But with the help of a guide like this, day trips by car can be another way to enjoy the county's scenery while also learning what's gone on here since ancient times. For those who lack the time or the physical ability to take long walks, we offer this book as a travel alternative.

Pembrokeshire's history is long and complex; the six tours in this book offer just a glimpse of what has occurred here over the past 6,000 years. The most intriguing and evocative reminders, of course, are the county's many ancient remnants, including hill forts, burial chambers, standing stones, and Celtic crosses. Archaeologists have counted an amazing 526 ancient monuments in Pembrokeshire, from the Stone Age to medieval times. Most are hidden in hedgerows or otherwise hard to find; our tours point out only those that can be easily seen or accessed from public roads.

No matter where you are in the county, you are never more than 10 miles from the sea or an estuary. The Welsh term for the county is *Sir Penfro*, and *penfro* means 'land's end'. Surrounded on three sides by water, Pembrokeshire has long been visited by seafaring peoples. Scholars now believe that the people we think of as the native Welsh began living here around 2000 BC. When the Romans took control of the area around AD 70, the locals eventually accepted them and life went on as usual, no doubt because the Romans found Pembrokeshire too remote to bother with. But there is increasing evidence that they were most definitely here, for at least 300 years.

After the Romans left, Irish tribes crossed the sea and founded colonies in northern Pembrokeshire; they helped usher in the Age of the Saints. Like the Romans, the Irish no doubt blended in with the local populations, probably ruling for about a century. They left behind a scattering of memorial stones inscribed with the Irish alphabet called Ogham. The area we now call Wales soon became a collection of feuding kingdoms.

Around AD 900, the Vikings began attacking the West Wales shores, setting up trading posts and kidnapping locals and making slaves of them. They left evidence of their presence in place names like Skomer, Caldey, Skokholm, Grassholm, and Gateholm islands and the town of Fishguard. But the feisty Welsh were able to prevent them from taking over.

The next to invade were the Normans, and they did take over in 1093, holding southern Pembrokeshire in particular and building a string of castles to keep the Welsh at bay. Nearly 200 years later, King Edward I of England claimed Wales as a colony. In 1536, England annexed Wales. It officially became part of Great Britain in 1707.

Those who wish to learn more about Pembrokeshire's past will find several good books on the topic, including: *Pembrokeshire: The Concise History* by Roger Turvey (University of Wales Press, 2006); *The Buildings of Wales: Pembrokeshire* (Yale University Press, 2004); *Saints and Stones* by Damian Walford Davies and Anne Eastman (Gomer, 2002) *Pembrokeshire: Journeys and Stories* by Trevor Fishlock and Jeremy Moore (Gomer Press, 2011).

We hope you enjoy exploring Pembrokeshire's back roads as much as we do. We wish to thank Mr. Vivian Thomas for his help in reviewing the tours; any errors are of course ours.

# Tour 1

## Tenby to Angle to Pembroke to Carew

*This tour visits three of the prettiest castles in Wales—Manorbier, Pembroke, and Carew—and passes by several glorious beaches. This is the longest tour, about 50 miles, but there is much to be seen and enjoyed. Either make an early start of it or split the tour into two days, especially if you are based in Tenby or Pembroke; then do the Pembroke to Tenby portion another day. (Also, be sure to plan on spending at least half a day seeing lovely Tenby.) There is no need to pack a lunch, for there are several good pubs and cafes along the way.*

**Tenby** (*Dinbych-y-pysgod*, meaning 'Little Fort of the Fish') is a picture-perfect Welsh holiday resort town. It's more colourful and atmospheric than a typical British seaside resort. Rows of pastel-painted Victorian townhouses line the hilly, curved streets. In the summer months, arrive early to find a place to park; the town is great for strolling, picture-taking, shopping, and eating.

Tenby is dramatically situated on a promontory, with views of the harbor on one side and a long, wide beach and the sea on the other. The town walls—from the 1200s and among the oldest and most complete walls in Britain—hint at a rich past. The town museum, located next to the Tenby castle tower ruins on Castle Hill, is small but well-done and full of interesting displays.

**Tenby houses**

---

### Caldey Island
A 20-minute boat ride from Tenby Harbour will take you to Caldey Island, home of the Reformed Order of Cistercian monks. The island's English name is of Viking origin; the Welsh name is Ynys Byr. The first structure here was a Celtic monastery in the 500s. The beautiful white abbey building was built between 1907 and 1915 in the Arts and Crafts style. The village shop sells lavender perfume, shortbread, and chocolate, all produced by the monks. Open Monday through Saturday from Easter through October (closed on Sundays, as well as certain Saturdays in April and October, phone 01834 844453, www.caldey-island.co.uk)

---

Tenby's sheltered location on Carmarthen Bay no doubt attracted its early residents. Stone tools dating from about 28,000 BC have been found in Hoyle's Cave near here, the earliest sign of humans in Pembrokeshire. Tenby itself was first mentioned in the Book of Taliesin in the 800s as a hill fort, probably of Norse origin.

Tenby became a trading town during Norman times. Its castle is long gone—today only the ruins of one small tower remain. The Normans built it in the late 1100s to protect the settlement from the (justifiably) angry Welsh natives, who had tried twice to get rid of the invaders. But the Normans held tight and later built the town walls in the 1200s for further protection. The unusual Five Arches gate you see today was built a few centuries later.

By the 1500s, Tenby was a busy port town, with ships arriving from Spain and Portugal. You can get a feel for Tenby's trade-oriented past by visiting the Tudor Merchant's House above the harbor. This narrow building has been restored by the National Trust to its medieval appearance and gives visitors an interesting look at Tenby's long and prosperous past (opening times vary; see www.nationaltrust.org.uk)

In 1512, a child was born in Tenby who would go on to have a most amazing career. Robert Recorde was a physician (it is said to King Edward VI and Queen Mary) and mathematician who was educated at both Oxford and Cambridge. He published the first book on algebra written in English and is credited with 'inventing' the equal sign. Perhaps his most imaginative contribution was the coining of a word to describe raising a number to the eight power: 'zenzizenzizenzic', or as he explained, it 'doeth represent the square of squares squaredly'. He is buried in St Mary's Church on High Street, also worth a visit; it dates to the 1200s.

By the 1640s, Cromwell had laid siege to Tenby, and the English Civil War took its toll. Then the Black Death hit a few years later and claimed the lives of perhaps half the townspeople. By the mid-1700s, Tenby had fallen into ruins.

But by the 1780s, a health craze for salt water baths and bathing in the sea began to bring Tenby back to life. In the early 1800s, a London banker named Sir William Paxton saw the potential and began developing Tenby as a holiday destination for the rich. It helped that the ongoing Napoleonic wars made tourist travel to most of Europe impractical, if not impossible. Still, to get to Tenby you had to really want to get away. The stagecoach from London took a grueling 29 hours each way. Rail service began in the 1860s, and Tenby blossomed after that.

The fort-looking building you see on St Catherine's Island— that stretch of land below Castle Hill that separates the two beach areas—was built around 1870 to deter a French invasion. Its name comes from the fact that a chapel to St Catherine stood on the spot in the Middle Ages. The fort was sold and converted into a private home around 1914, and in 1940 the structure was taken over by the Army as a garrison. After WW II, it was sold and briefly turned into a zoo. It is undergoing restoration and is open on most weekends for tours.

> *Leave Tenby on the A4139 by following the signs marked Pembroke, heading west from town toward the Tenby Golf Course. About 7 minutes out of town, shortly after passing through the village of Lydstep (site of the sixth century Penally Abbey, now in ruins), turn left at the sign for Manorbier, B4585.*
>
> *In about a mile, you will pass through the small village of Manorbier. Veer left at the sign for Manorbier Beach, and shortly you will see the car park for the castle on the left. From there, walk up the sidewalk back up toward the village and look across the street for an iron gate with a sign that says Secret Entrance. Cross the street and go up the short flight of steps and onto the path to the castle. (As you walk toward the castle entrance, you can see above the car park the ancient Church of St James, a twelfth-century Norman church.)*
>
> *Accessibility note: There is level access to the castle from the village; no parking is available, but there is room to drop off passengers.*

**Manorbier Castle** may look familiar to you if you have seen the 2003 movie 'I Capture the Castle' or the BBC's 1989 production of 'The Lion, the Witch, and the Wardrobe'.

**Manorbier Castle**

**View of the sea from Manorbier tower**

Like so many Welsh castles, this one began as a motte and bailey. It was built in the late 1000s by Odo de Barri, a Norman knight. He had been given land in this area in return for his help in taking Pembrokeshire in 1000. His son, William de Barri, began building the stone castle in the early 1100s.

William's fourth son, the famous Welsh scholar Gerald de Barri—Geraldus Cambrensis or Gerald of Wales—was born in the castle in 1146. He later wrote of his birthplace, 'In all the broad lands of Wales, Manorbier is the most pleasant place by far'. It would indeed have been a fabulous place to live. Don't miss climbing up the southwest tower for a grand view.

The castle was severely damaged in 1645, during the English Civil War, and fell into ruin over the next two centuries. It was privately and partially restored in 1880. The walls are medieval as are some of the rooms; the rest dates to the 1500s and 1600s and modern times. Although privately owned, it is open to the public daily, April through September. There is plenty to see and explore here, offering visitors a glimpse into life in medieval times (phone 01834 871394, manorbiercastle.co.uk).

*Turn right out of the car park, go up the hill the way you came, and make a sharp left turn almost immediately. Stay left toward the winding road sign and return to the main road, A4139, and turn left toward Pembroke. Stay on this road, passing through Jameston and Hodgeston.*

*Go through the village of Lamphey, then take a right turn following the brown signs to Lamphey Bishops Palace, then take an almost immediate left following another sign to the palace, down a narrow lane that leads to a resort hotel. Park in the area across from the palace entrance.*

**Lamphey Bishop's Palace**

**Lamphey Bishop's Palace** should not be missed. The bishops of St Davids built the first structures, the Old Hall and the Western Hall, in the 1200s. Then, in the mid-1300s, Bishop Henry de Gower added the dramatic east block; he was also responsible for the Bishop's Palace at St Davids. There is no doubt the bishops who retreated here lived a good life.

It is said that the father of King Henry VII, Edmund Tudor, Earl of Richmond, enjoyed staying here when he was traveling in the area (his brother Jasper was the Earl of Pembroke, and both were descendants of the Welsh hero Rhys ap Gruffydd).

Edmund and his young bride (she was 12!), Margaret Beaufort, may have stayed at Lamphey in 1455. She was a descendant of Edward III, and the reason for Henry's later claim to the crown. Their only child, the future king, was born in January 1457 in nearby Pembroke Castle, just three months after Edmund's death from the plague after being captured during the War of the Roses.

From the 1500s until the late 1600s, Lamphey Bishop's Palace became Crown property; then it fell into private hands. Fortunately the later owners maintained the ruins. Royal Air Force and U.S. troops camped on the grounds during WW II.

CADW took it over in 1925. It is open daily year-round (phone 01646 672224, cadw.wales.gov.uk).

*Leave the palace and return to the main road. Turn right, then immediately left, onto A4139, Freshwater East Road. After a short distance, turn right onto B4584, following signs to Freshwater East. In less than 5 minutes, follow the sign for Freshwater East Beach.*

You are now on Stackpole Road. **Freshwater East Beach** will soon be on the left, with parking on the right. This beach has easy access, and toilets are located on the short path to the beach.

*Continue to Stackpole on this single-track road. In about 5 minutes, you will pass a sign to Barafundle Beach—don't turn here unless you plan to go to the beach. But it is one of Britain's most beautiful beaches, so if you have time you may want to stop; see the sidebar below. (Parking charges apply at this National Trust property, March to October until 17:30, free other times, and then make the half-mile walk to the beach.)*

*Next you will pass through Stackpole village. As you leave the village, you will enter a curvy, wooded road. On the way you will pass the entrance to Stackpole Court, another National Trust pay and display car park with alternate access to Barafundle and Bosherston Lakes.*

---

### Barafundle Beach

This was once the private beach of a large and elegant Palladian villa, Stackpole Court, once the largest house in Wales. It was torn down in 1963. The owners from the late 1700s until 1978 were the Cawdor family of the Stackpole estate. They built the steep flights of steps down to this wide, pristine, golden sand beach. You can take the steps back up at the far side and take a scenic walk along the cliffs to Bosherston Lakes, which were created in the 1800s as garden features for Stackpole Court. From there you can return to the Barafundle car park via a flat farm road. Allow at least two or three hours.

---

*In a few minutes you will come to yield sign. Turn left, following the signs for Castlemartin and **Bosherston**. You are now on B4319. Turn left at the next sign to Bosherton.*

*Bosherston has a pub and a cafe. Continue past Bosherston and stay on road to the right to St Govans. You will pass by the lane leading to Broad Haven beach.*

Shortly you will enter the **Castlemartin** military firing range, which is closed when the red flag is flying to signify live firing exercises; however, the road is always open on weekends and public holidays.

The road ends at the car park (free, no facilities) at **St Govan's**; note the signs pointing to the short level path to see the chapel. There is a steep flight of steps down to the chapel, but it can be seen quite well from the cliffs on the left.

It is thought that St Govan was a sixth-century monk from Ireland who came to Wales for unknown reasons in his later years. The story goes that he was being pursued by pirates. As he was looking around for a hiding place, a fissure in the cliffside miraculously opened. He ended up living in a nearby cave for the rest of his life. The chapel that is so neatly nestled in the rocks far below was probably built over the cave St Govan occupied in the 1200s.

*There are beautiful views of the coast in both directions from here, with easy walking on dirt and grass paths. From the St Govan's car park, head back to Bosherston and turn left to return to the main road. At the T-junction, turn left on to B4319 to go toward Castlemartin and Freshwater West.*

*NOTE*: If the red flag is flying, you will not be able to take the following route to see the Stack Rocks and the Green Bridge of Wales. Instead, you will have to follow the diversion, which will take you to the next set of directions, at Castlemartin. If you must take the diversion, note that there is a public spectator area on the road if you wish to watch the firing exercises.

**St Govan's chapel**

In about three minutes, after passing through Merrion, you will see a sign on the left pointing to **Stack Rocks**, which are just a short drive down the lane. Also at this stop is the famous **Green Arch of Wales.** There is free parking here, but no other facilities, and the access to both sites (the Stack Rocks are to the left, and the Green Arch is up to the right) is easy to walk; everything can be seen from the top of the cliffs. Don't let your children run loose up here, though.

This road continues to pass through the Castlemartin firing range, a 6,000-acre training site operated by the British Army. The government took the land from the Cawdor's enormous Stackpole Estate in 1938 to use for tank training and live-firing practice.

Physically, this area is unlike any other part of Pembrokeshire, in part because the natural vegetation has returned now that the farms are gone. People have lived here even before the farms, as evidenced by the remains of Iron Age promontory forts along the cliff tops.

*As you enter the village of Castlemartin, follow the sign at the roundabout for Freshwater West to stay on B4319.*

High dunes with tall grasses dominate this narrow but wonderfully scenic road. In the distance to the right you will see the stacks of the oil refineries in Milford Haven. Soon the magnificent beach of **Freshwater West** will appear on the left. You may want to look for the petrified trees on the beach at low tide. This beach is said to be the best surfing beach in Wales. There is easy access on a paved path down to the beach, and toilets and free parking are available.

> *Leaving Freshwater West, continue on the single-track road and turn left at the sign for Angle onto B4320. In about three minutes, turn right at another sign for Angle. Shortly, turn left into the village. Take the first sharp right, at the sign on the side of a building pointing toward the Old Point House. After you cross a small stone bridge across the tidal creek, look to the left to see a medieval Norman tower.*

The **Angle** tower was in fact a residence, now known as the Old Rectory or the Tower House. The main entrance was on the first floor and was entered via a drawbridge over a moat. The upper rooms even had fireplaces. It was no doubt built as a safe place for a well-to-do family, perhaps the de Shirburns. Nothing particularly historic has ever happened here, so far as anyone knows. It was restored in 1999 and is open to the public; do watch your step.

**Tower House, Angle**

The origin of Angle's name is not certain, but it could have come from the fact that it was located in an angle or nook, 'in angulo'. Or it may have been named after early landowners here, the de Nangles, particularly since the town has also been called 'Nangle'.

People have lived in this area, on the Milford Haven estuary, since about 4000 BC. The Devils' Quoit burial chamber, located 1.5 miles southeast, dates to around 3000 BC. The town has several interesting ruins dating to medieval times, including a 'nunnery', a fisherman's chapel, a dovecote, and a windmill.

*From the Tower House, turn around and go back toward the town. Turn right at the intersection. Pass through the town and continue on to West Angle Bay.*

On the right just out of town is a sign pointing right to the Chapel Bay Fort and Museum (open Easter to October, Fridays through Sundays 10 am to 4 pm). The fort was operational from 1817 until 1932; the museum's volunteers explain military technology and weaponry through the ages.

**West Angle Bay Beach** will soon come into view, with the old fort in the distance off to the right. This national park beach (free parking, a cafe and toilets) is a wide sandy beach in a lovely sheltered location, perfect for children to swim and explore its tidal pools. Across the water is the village of Dale.

*Return to Angle village and turn left at the yield sign toward Pembroke. Continue straight at the junction toward Pembroke; you are now on B4320, which will become B4319 as you approach Pembroke.*

In about 10 to 15 minutes, you will enter **Pembroke** *(Penfro)*. Follow the signs to the town centre. Castle parking is on your left, and soon Pembroke Castle will come into view. This castle is one of the largest and most important in Wales. It sits high on a promontory above the Cleddau estuary, which forms a natural, if partial, moat.

Pembroke's location had strategic importance to the Normans, who founded the town in 1102. It became a major port for ships to Ireland. But for a long time after, Pembroke struggled economically, and by the 1500s it had only 64 householders. It began to come back to life as a port and market town in the early 1700s, and by the 1800s many of the homes and buildings you see today along the main street had been built.

# Pembrokeshire Backroads

The first stone structures of Pembroke Castle, replacing the earthen and wood defences of a century earlier, were built by William Marshal, Earl of Pembroke, beginning in 1189. It was well constructed—something the native Welsh, including forces lead by Owain Glyndwr, discovered. They attacked it many times, unsuccessfully, over the next 200 years.

As described earlier in this tour, Jasper Tudor—half-brother of Henry VI and then Earl of Pembroke—took his brother Edmund's widow under his protection in the castle, where in 1457 she gave birth to the child who would become Henry VII, the first of the Tudor kings. Henry was half English, one-quarter French, and one-quarter Welsh.

During the English Civil War, Oliver Cromwell attacked Pembroke Castle for several weeks in 1648. The inhabitants finally surrendered, having been starved into defeat. Cromwell later destroyed portions of the castle so it could never be used in war again. For the next three centuries, it fell into decay and served as a convenient stone quarry for the locals.

Interestingly, the castle was built over a very large cavern, which is reached by a tight spiral staircase. Flint tools from the Mesolithic period have been found here.

In 1879, Joseph Cobb, a lawyer and investor in railways from Brecon, began restoring Pembroke Castle; he also restored Manorbier Castle. Today a private charitable trust owns it, and it is open daily (01646 684585, pembroke-castle.co.uk).

**Pembroke Castle**

*Leaving the castle, the main road takes you through the centre of town. At the traffic signal, turn left at the sign marked St Clears, A4075. In about 5 minutes, this road intersects the A477. Turn right toward St Clears.*

*Shortly, you will pass through Milton and see a brown sign for Carew Castle pointing to the left. Turn left at the roundabout onto A4075 to go the short distance to Carew Castle and Tidal Mill.*

Before there was a castle here, along the Carew River, there probably were Iron Age forts. It is a flat, lovely setting, a little unusual for West Wales. Over time, the medieval fort that was first built here became a Tudor palace and then an Elizabethan house.

Gerald of Windsor built **Carew Castle** as a 'branch' castle to Pembroke Castle beginning around 1100. Like Pembroke, it was then an earthen and timber structure. Gerald's wife was the beautiful Nest, daughter of Rhys ap Tewdwr (for more about Nest, see Tour 5). The stone structures probably came later, beginning in the late 1200s.

In 1480 Carew came into the hands of Rhys ap Thomas, who had fought for Henry VII at the Battle of Bosworth and became prominent in southwest Wales as a result. He renovated the castle in the early 1500s. His heir, his grandson Rhys ap Gruffydd, never inherited the castle because Henry VIII accused him of treason and ordered his execution.

**Carew Castle**

13

In 1558, the castle came into the hands of Sir John Perrot, the most powerful person in Pembrokeshire at the time (and rumored to be an illegitimate son of Henry VIII). He tore down a tower and part of a curtain wall and added the glorious north wing, with its stunning rows of mullioned windows. Perrot faced the same fate as the previous owner. He was convicted of treason and died in the Tower of London in 1592. The Carew family bought the castle back and lived there until the 1680s, when its slow decline began.

It is worth making the walk to the tidal mill, the foundations of which probably date to medieval times. The current four-storey building was erected in the mid-1800s. The equipment is still intact.

The impressive carved Celtic cross along the roadside in the village is a copy of the 11th-century original. It probably commemorates the death of Maredudd ap Edwin, a ruler of West Wales, and is considered one of the finest Dark Age monuments in Britain.

**Carew Cross**

*The tour ends here.*

*Return to the A477 and follow the sign to St Clears. At the next roundabout, follow the sign to B4318 if you wish to return to Tenby.*

# Tour 2

# Haverfordwest to Little Haven to Solva

*This tour, of about 24 miles, begins in Haverfordwest, the county town of Pembrokeshire County. Straddling the Western Cleddau River, it is the county's largest town and has been a major crossroads for centuries, ever since the Normans (or perhaps Tancred the Fleming) built a castle here in the 1100s. It then heads south along the coast and ends up in the picturesque village of Solva.*

Four Welsh heroes—Gruffydd ap Rhys (in 1135-36), Llewelyn the Great (1220), Llewelyn the Last (1257), and Owain Glyndwr (1405)—all tried unsuccessfully to take the castle in **Haverfordwest** (*Hwlffordd*). But its position on a high ridge, plus the town wall that once surrounded it, made it fairly impenetrable. Cromwell, though, succeeded in 1645 and destroyed much of it, and then had the gall to order the townspeople to tear down the rest. Just the shell is left today. The citizens left enough behind to form the quarters for the town prison, which operated between 1779 and 1820.

The Town Museum on Castle Hill, on the castle grounds, has many interesting displays and is nicely laid out, well worth an hour's visit. It is open from late March through October, Monday through Saturday. (phone 01437 763087, www.haverfordwest-town-museum.org.uk)

The Welsh often pronounce Haverfordwest as 'Harford'. It was derived from an Old English word meaning "where the fat cows (heifers) forded the river'. The suffix '–west' was added,

**Haverfordwest Castle**

apparently, to avoid confusion with Hereford in England. Early on, it was also called Castleton.

Many Iron Age artifacts and Roman coins—including one minted in AD 91—have been found here, suggesting that people have lived in the area for a very long time. By the 1300s, there were perhaps as many as 5,000 inhabitants. By then it had become an important trade and manufacturing center, with ten guilds operating. But the Black Death struck in 1348, and the population declined by half or more. The town didn't begin to recover until the 1700s.

Haverfordwest claims to be the only Welsh town to have three parish churches. They all date to medieval times: St Martin's (the earliest, built in the 1100s), St Mary's, and St Thomas's.

The town has seen its share of conflict from Norman times on. It changed hands five times during the English Civil War in the mid-1600s and was even bombed once by the Germans in 1940, fortunately without causing any casualties.

*Follow the signs from the town center to A4076, Milford Haven. At the next roundabout, follow the Milford Haven sign. As you cross the bridge, look quickly to the right to see the ruins of the Haverfordwest Priory.*

The ruins here are what is left of an early 1200s Augustinian priory. The buildings were largely destroyed during the

Dissolution in the 1500s. Excavations in the late 1900s revealed some interesting artifacts, which are on display in the Town Museum.

This priory, alongside the Western Cleddau River, is unique in Britain because of its medieval-style raised-bed garden, which has been restored and maintained by CADW. The location is Union Hill, at the end of Quay Street. If you wish to visit it, ask at the Town Museum or at the tourist office downtown for directions. Admission is free and the site is open year-round, 10 am to 4 pm.

Also in this area, less than a mile past the priory (but not visible from the road), are the ruins of a grand mansion called Haroldston, built by the Harold family in the late 1300s. Enlarged by the Perrot family between the mid-1400s and late 1700s, it was one of the most magnificent homes in Britain at that time. But by the 1800s, it had been left to decay. It sits on private land today.

Sir John Perrot was a colorful character who was born at Haroldston in 1528. The rumor that he was an illegitimate child of Mary Berkeley and King Henry VIII is apparently without substance, but much talked about nonetheless. He was educated at St David's and had an illustrious career; he was knighted by King Edward I in 1547. He served as High Sheriff of Pembrokeshire, then mayor of Haverfordwest, and then Lord Deputy of Ireland, not to mention being the owner of Carew (see Tour 1) and Laugharne castles. He died in 1592 in the Tower of London, where he had had been imprisoned for treason, a charge probably trumped up by his enemies.

*At the next roundabout, Merlin's Bridge, stay on A4076 to Milford Haven/Johnston. When you come to the second roundabout in Johnston, take the exit to Tiers Cross.*

*At the next roundabout, Tiers Cross, follow the signs for Dale/Broadhaven. Then take a quick right just after the roundabout to Walwyn's Castle. This is a lovely country lane, despite the single track, and there are plenty of laybys. Stay on this for a couple of miles. At the T-junction, turn left at the yield sign and drive into the church car park directly ahead.*

## Milford Haven

Not on the tour, but an easy four-mile detour south of Johnston on A4076, is the town of Milford Haven, the second-largest in the county. The town is quite young by Welsh standards. It was founded in the 1790s as a potential whaling port, originally settled by about 50 American Quakers from Massachusetts who were looking for new opportunities. That venture didn't pan out, but the town grew steadily over the next two centuries. The Milford Haven Museum, housed in the 1794 Customs House on the waterfront, is well-done and worth a visit.

The Milford Haven waterway forms a natural harbor, one of the deepest natural harbours in the world. It has been important militarily and commercially for a long, long time. Ruins of Bronze Age and Iron Age promontory forts have been found near Dale, at the entrance to the waterway. St. Ann's Head, on the Dale Peninsula, was where Henry Tudor landed in 1485 on his way to the Battle of Bosworth, where he gained the British crown as King Henry VII. Cromwell left from here in 1649 for his invasion of Ireland. Today ferries cross to Rosslare, Ireland, from here.

The arrival of the railway in the 1860s increased the port's business. In the early 1900s it became home to one of the largest fishing fleets in Britain, but overfishing eventually ended that role. During WW II the Royal Air Force built the Sunderlands flying boat base nearby, and the U.S. Navy also built a base, to prepare LSTs for the Normandy Invasion.

In the late 1950s, oil refineries were built here, which changed the appearance of the area forever.

This is St James Church, in the village of **Walwyn's Castle**. The base of the steeple is built of lovely old stones. Walk through the gate into the churchyard and look left past the cemetery and you will see a stone stile next to a wooden gate, Climb over the stile, say hello to the sheep, and watch your step as you walk up the hill to see the castle earthworks.

These earthworks, parts of which can be easily seen, were begun in the 1100s, perhaps over the remains of yet another Iron Age hill fort. There was probably a stone tower here, but if other stones made up this 'castle' they are long gone. This was a well-sited and long-running operation. From 1247, it was the administrative center for the barony of Walwyn's Castle, part of the Lordship of Haverfordwest. The story goes that King Arthur's nephew, Gawain, was buried here.

> *Turn left out of the church car park and continue on this lane for 1.5 miles; you will pass a large poultry farm, Capestone. Stay on the road to Little Haven from here. Stay straight and follow signs for Little Haven/Talbenny. At the next T-junction, turn right to Talbenny/Little Haven. You will soon come to a main intersection; stay straight, following signs for Little Haven/Talbenny. In Talbenny, turn right.*

Just after you pass a large farm, Upper Talbenny, look to the left for the Church of St Mary the Virgin. Sitting on a ridge above St Brides Bay, the original church was built in the 1400 or 1500s; it was restored in the 1800s. Inside is a plaque dedicated to the 82 WW II servicemen who lost their lives flying missions from the nearby Talbenny RAF field. Talbenny was one of ten WW II airfields in Pembrokeshire.

**St James Church, Walwyn's Castle**

**Iron Age Hill Forts**
You will have passed  Romans Castle as the tour
headed to Walwyn's Castle. It is one of those
ancient Iron Age hill forts that appear as
numerous features on the Pembrokeshire
Ordnance Survey maps but can be infuriatingly
hard to find, not to mention that trespassing is
often involved. This entire area is full of ancient
remains, most all of them on private property
and hidden from view. It is best for one's sanity
(and we speak from experience) to be content
with the fact that while on this drive you will
have passed it. It was not Roman at all—its
original name was Ramus. It was roughly
pentagonal in shape and had good views to the
coast. It is now part of a farm pasture and has
been much disturbed by farming over the
centuries.

*Soon there will be another sign for Little Haven. Turn left
toward Little Haven.*

As the road drops into **Little Haven**, you will have good views
of the sea and a lovely wide beach will appear. This charming
little village is a good place to stop for a quick look around and
a snack or meal at one of several cafes. This village and the
next, Broad Haven, developed as beach resort towns in the
early 1800s. Several old houses from that early period still
stand. Coal was once mined in the nearby cliffs.

*Go through Little Haven and make a sharp left turn at the
sign to Broad Haven. Continue through Broad Haven
along the sea. Follow the signs for Nolton, veering left up
the hill out of the village.*

*In about 7 minutes, stay straight at the give-way sign
junction, following the sign to Simpson Cross. At the
junction with A487, turn left toward Roch and St Davids.
In a little over a mile, watch for the right turn that will
take you into Roch. (It is just across from a covered bus
stop.) You can hardly miss seeing the large castle tower*

*on the right as you approach Roch. After the turn, stay straight on Church Road into the village. Soon the castle will be up the hill on the left. It is now a stylish luxury hotel.*

Dating to the 1200s, the striking tower of **Roch Castle** can be seen for miles around. It was built by a Norman knight named Adam de Rupe. 'Roch' comes from the French word for rock, *roche*, and it is obvious that this castle rises out of the rock that forms its foundation. Its purpose may have been to serve as a defence along the Landsker Line—the imaginary line dividing 'English' Wales and 'Welsh' Wales dating back to Norman times (see the sidebar on the next page.

Later owners were the Walter family. The castle was burned in 1644 during the English civil war and remained a ruin for more than 300 years until it was purchased and restored in 1900. In 1977, it was turned into a rental holiday home, and in 2009 a new owner completely revamped it and turned it into a hotel.

The nearby church is St Mary's, built between 1857 and 1865 on the site of a 1200s church.

*Turn around and return to A487, and turn right.*

**Roch Castle**

You will soon pass through another picturesque beach town, **Newgale**. Continue through Newgale to Solva. Lower Solva's only car park on the A487 is off to the left at the harbour area. There are numerous shops and cafes in the village.

---

**The Landsker Line**
Landsker, which is an old Anglo-Saxon word meaning a visible boundary, doesn't really fit its meaning as applied to Pembrokeshire. Here it refers to an invisible language and cultural boundary between the historically English-speaking (south of the line) and Welsh-speaking (north of the line) areas. As long ago as 1603, when the writer George Owen apparently coined the term, the area south of the line has been called Anglia Transwalliana or 'Little England beyond Wales'. The line itself—which runs from Newgale in the west through Roch and Llawhaden to Laugharne Castle in the east—goes back hundreds of years before then, when the Normans invaded southwest Wales in the 1100s and began building their many castles, the purpose of which was to control the irate Welsh. The line has moved back and forth a bit over the centuries. Today there are still many more native Welsh speakers in the northern part of the county.

---

**Solva** *(Solfach)* is a picturesque port and popular tourist destination, with great views of St Brides Bay from the Pembrokeshire Coast Path that runs above the village. Solva has two parts, Upper and Lower. Upper Solva contains most of the homes and cottages; Lower Solva, on a single street, sits at the end of a deep and narrow inlet, with a well-protected harbour.

Solva has been a port since the Middle Ages. In the late 1800s, ten lime kilns were operating here, and you can see remains of a few of them along the harbour. The Pembrokeshire Coast Path is accessible from the parking area.

The high ridge to the left of the harbor is known as the Gribin, and it was the site of three Iron Age forts. Several other ancient ruins can be seen along the cliff tops above Solva. For hundreds of years, St Brides Bay was a lawless area, favored by smugglers and pirates.

*The tour ends in Solva.*

About a mile north of Solva, on the tight little road heading out of town in the other direction from the harbor, is the Solva Woolen Mill, in the hamlet of **Middle Mill,** on the Solva River. This working mill is worth a detour to visit, as it is one of only two surviving mills in Pembrokeshire (the other is described in Tour 3). In 1900, the county had 26 such mills. This mill was once owned by Tom Griffiths, who moved it here from St Davids in 1907. It was powered by a 10-foot overshot wheel. In recent years, the mill has turned to weaving rugs, stair carpet, and blankets; its gift shop sells woolen articles from other parts of Britain as well.

**Solva harbour**

23

# Tour 3

## St Davids to Porthgain to Fishguard

*This tour begins in the city of St Davids and is short in distance—only about 20 miles along an especially gorgeous stretch of the West Wales coastline—but long in history and scenic beauty. You should allow most of a day for it. There's no need to pack a lunch, for there are several good cafes and pubs in the area; the seaside village of Porthgain makes an especially good lunch stop about halfway if you get an early start in St Davids.*

*There is parking near the cathedral, and plenty more across the street from the St Davids visitor center, Oriel y Parc, at the other end of town (toward Solva on A487).*

This rugged part of Pembrokeshire has been a favoured place to live since Neolithic times. It may even have been the location of a Roman port called Menevia, but so far no remains have been unearthed. The fact that portions of a Roman road running between here and Carmarthen (also known as the Bishop's Road, mentioned below) have been discovered lend credence to the possibility. Irish colonists arrived here in the 400s, not long after the Romans left Britain.

**St Davids** *(Tyddewi)* was named for the patron saint of Wales, the monk known as *Dewi Sant*, who was born sometime in the early 500s. Nothing is known for sure about him. The story goes that David's mother, Non, was a Welsh woman who gave birth to him during a terrible storm above the coast near here; his father, it is claimed, was a prince of Ceredigion. He is credited with spreading Christianity throughout western

Britain. He was made a Catholic saint around 1120. St David's feast day is March 1 and is celebrated as a major Welsh holiday around the world, in Welsh communities from Argentina to the United States.

The monks of his order followed a simple, ascetic life; his followers ate no meat and drank only water. His symbol was the leek, which has long been the national symbol of Wales, along with the daffodil.

In the 1100s, the pope at the time decreed that two pilgrimages to St Davids were equal to one to Rome, and three were equivalent to one journey to Jerusalem. If you entered St Davids from the east, on the A487 from Solva, you will have followed the pilgrims' route along the ancient 'Bishop's Road', which has so far been uncovered from here to Wiston (Tour 6).

St Davids is not much larger than a good-sized village, but officially it is called a 'city'—the smallest in Wales—because it has a cathedral. (Queen Elizabeth II conferred the honor in 1995, reinstating the earlier honor granted in the 1500s.)

Visiting the cathedral is a must. Today's core was built by the Normans beginning sometime after the 1180s, on the foundations of earlier churches and St David's original monastery. This area was a popular spot for frequent Viking attacks in the 900s and 1000s, and they destroyed earlier structures here.

If you parked in the car park down the road from the cathedral, follow the signs to the footpath to get to the cathedral and the Bishop's Palace ruins. If you parked at Oriel y Parc, walk up High Street to the small square with the tall Celtic cross and head down the hill on The Pebbles, following the signs. (The cathedral's unusual location, in a low-lying valley created by the River Alun, was probably chosen to better hide it from marauders.)The cathedral is uniquely beautiful inside, so don't miss seeing it.

Buried at the cathedral are possibly the bones of St David and St Justinian; Edmund Tudor, father of King Henry VII; and Bishop Henry Gower, who was an early builder of this church as well as Lamphey Bishop's Palace (see Tour 1).

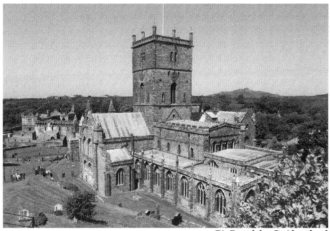

**St Davids Cathedral**

Near the cathedral you will see signs to nearby St Non's Chapel ruins, also worth a visit; you can walk or drive (though the lane is quite narrow). Our main driving tour, however, continues toward St Justinian and Whitesands beach.

*From the cathedral area, follow the signs to St Justinian and St Davids Lifeboat Station. Soon, veer to the left to follow the sign to Treginnis. Drive for about a mile, then turn right to follow the sign for St Justinian. Where the road begins to turn left rather sharply, you will see a large rock outcropping and a driveway to a holiday farmhouse. If you wish to stop, park in the small layby on the right.*

You are at the base of a hill known as **Clegyr Boia**. There is an overgrown path leading to the top of the outcropping. It is a short way up and not difficult. If you don't mind the brambles, walk up and enjoy the views on a clear day.

Clegyr Boia is thought to be another of the many Iron Age hill forts in the area. But excavations in the early part of the twentieth century revealed two Neolithic house foundations (rather unusual for this part of Wales) on the top of the hill, dating to 5,000 or 6,000 years ago. This hill was named after Boia, a chieftain (or perhaps pirate) from Ireland who ruled this area in the 500s, during the time of St David (legend suggests that the two men did not get along).

### St Justinian
The legend goes that St Justinian was a sixth-century Christian missionary who came from Brittany; he had left there after being commanded by God to withdraw from the world. He set sail in a coracle to Ramsey Island, where he built a cell and lived as a hermit. He later became a friend, teacher, and associate of St David.

The chapel was built in the 14th century on the site of a much older shrine and was restored in the early sixteenth-century by Bishop Vaughan. Although the roof is gone, the structure is still intact

Several legends are associated with St Justinian. One suggests that he was murdered on Ramsey Island. His harsh regime had become impossible to bear, and his followers cut off his head. St Justinian then managed to swim to the mainland clutching his head and came ashore at what is now called St Justinian's Point, the spot where he wanted to be buried. Through divine retribution, it is said that the murderers contracted leprosy and were banished to an outcrop off Ramsey Island known as Lepers' Rock.

**The view from Clegyr Boia toward St Davids**

*From Clegyr Boia, drive to the T-junction and either turn left to see the St Davids lifeboat launch and the chapel ruins (and Ramsey Island across the way), or turn right to continue the tour. You will now be heading back in the direction of St Davids. Veer left at the fork in the road at the next junction and continue driving left toward Whitesands Beach. Soon, the craggy hill called **Carn Llidi** will appear ahead. At the T-junction, turn left toward Whitesands beach. Stay on this road to see the beach and perhaps take a walk in the area.*

A path near the car park leads up to the top of Carn Llidi from **Whitesands Bay** beach. Those who make the trek will be rewarded with incredible land and sea views for miles around. You can also walk (be sure to have a map or ask other walkers for directions) to a 5,000-year-old burial chamber known as Coetan Arthur, not to be confused with Coetan Carreg Arthur in Newport (Tour 4).

*From the Whitesands car park, go back toward the way you came, and at the next give-way sign at the T-junction, turn left on the B4583 toward Llanrhian, Porthgain, and Trefin. In 4.5 miles, after the hamlet of Berea, at the junction is a small sign pointing to Abereiddy. Turn here if you wish to visit this interesting part of the coast (see the sidebar, next page).Otherwise, continue on to Porthgain on the B4583. In Llanrhian, turn left at the sign for Porthgain and make the short drive into the village.*

29

## Aberreidy

Aberreidy is a popular coasteering and diving spot because of the Blue Lagoon, a flooded slate quarry. (Its striking blue-green color is caused by minerals.) The beach itself, with a large car park, is picturesque and on the Pembrokeshire Coast Path. The two-mile walk—fairly level with a few steep spots—along the cliff-tops to Porthgain is one of the most scenic in Wales. To see the Blue Lagoon, walk up the hill to the right.

**Porthgain** (Welsh meaning 'beautiful port') is a rare remnant of West Wales' industrial past, dating back to the 1850s. A tramway once connected the port here with slate quarries located here and in Trefin and Aberreidy. Water-powered mills here were used to slice the slate—used for roofs—before shipment. As slate production decreased, the village turned to brickmaking, using the waste from the slate, and then to stone crushing for use in road building, until the 1930s. The stone, an exceptionally hard variety of volcanic rock called dolerite, came from quarries nearby. The bins you see there today were used to separate the crushed rock into various sizes.

A lime kiln also still stands, on the right side of the road to the harbor area. The two white structures you see at the tops of the cliffs on either side of the harbor are basically lighthouses without the lights, once used to guide ships into this secluded little harbor. The Coast Path passes above the village.

**Porthgain harbour**

## Tour 3: St Davids to Porthgain to Fishguard

Today Porthgain is a fishing village, and fishermen catch crabs and lobsters here for shipment all over Europe. It is also a popular tourist destination, with a pub that dates back to the 1700s, a good fish and chips café, and quality art galleries. A pamphlet describing more of the area history and a self-guided walk is available in the shops.

*From Porthgain, return to the main road (B4583). At the first main junction, turn left toward* **Trefin***. Immediately on your left is the Llanrhian church, said to possess a 15th-century font from Jerusalem.*

*Continue on the road to Trefin. In Trefin, follow the signs pointing left for Abercastle.*

*About a half mile out of Trefin, on the left, is Longhouse Farm. Below the sign, there a small wooden walker's sign pointing to Carreg Samson. Turn down the lane into the farm, head to the right and look past the gate past the big metal roofed barn to see the Carreg Samson burial chamber in the field. It is a short walk down a concrete lane to the stones.*

**Carreg Samson** is a Neolithic tomb some 5,000 years old. Once a ring of stones would have surrounded it. Like nearby Pentre Ifan, excavations have revealed that it was erected over a pit that had been filled in, for unknown reasons. It got its name from the legend that St Samson used a single finger to place the capstone.

**Carreg Samson**

Beyond the tomb, on the cliffs above the sea in the distance are the remains of an Iron Age fort called Castell Coch. Two other similar forts sit along this area of coastline.

*Return to the road and turn left to continue toward Abercastle. You will pass up and through this small village. After several minutes, you will enter **Mathry**. Drive through the village to the intersection with A487 and turn left to go toward Fishguard.*

*In less than two miles, turn left at the sign pointing to the Melin Tregwynt Woolen Mill (see the sidebar next page) and Abermawr.*

If you detour to **Abermawr**, you will see a gorgeous beach today, but it could have looked much different: after the Navy refused to let Isambard Kingdom Brunel build a ferry port to Ireland in Fishguard, Brunel proposed to build it here at Abermawr, at what would have been the terminus of his Great Western Railway. Thankfully, that plan was also abandoned.

*Continue through the hamlet of **Granston**. Turn right at the first sign for the woolen mill and St Nicholas.*

*At the next intersection, turn left if you wish to visit the woolen mill. Otherwise, continue on to the next intersection, and turn left to enter St Nicholas.*

The standing stones near the parish church in **St Nicholas** underscore its importance as a religious site, perhaps dating back to the fifth century.

**St Nicholas Church**

## Tregwynt Treasures

The Melin Tregwynt Woolen Mill, more than 200 years old, is one of two working mills (the other is Solva, in Middle Mill) left in Pembrokeshire (once there were dozens). It makes a good spot to take a break for refreshments and a little history, as well as do some shopping.

The mill was once part of the vast estate of Tregwynt Mansion, about a half mile from Granston and built in the 1700s. Except for one period, ending in 1986, the Harries family has owned this estate for about six centuries. In 1797, a ball was going on in the mansion when news came of the 'invasion' by French troops (more about this later in this tour) at nearby Carreg Wastad Point.

In 1996, an even more exciting event happened at the mansion. During excavations for a tennis court, some 500 gold and silver coins from the 1500s and 1600s were uncovered. It is thought they were hidden about 1648, during the difficult times in Pembrokeshire during the English Civil War. The British Museum now holds the collection, called the Tregwynt Hoard.

*As you enter **St Nicholas**, take the first left and you will see the car park for the village hall (which is directly behind the church).*

Park at the hall and walk down the lane to the church entrance, which faces the lane. If you are lucky, it will be unlocked. Inside are three inscribed stones from the Dark Ages set in the chancel, one of which unusually commemorates a woman: *Tunccetace uxsor of Daari hic iacit,* which means 'Tunccetace, wife of Daarus, lies here.'

*Continue driving past the church to return to the main road and turn left. In a few minutes you will pass through Trefasser. The volcanic outcropping of Garn Fawr appears ahead in the distance.*

**Garn Fawr**

*At the next junction, veer to the right, following the signs
for Fishguard. Shortly, at the sign for Strumble Head, turn
left.*

**Garn Fawr**—the jagged peak that is home to the impressive
remains of three Iron Age hill forts—is now just ahead. The
road becomes a narrow lane. There is a car park near the top
of the hill on the left, should you want to walk up paths to to
top. This area also contains several chambered burial sites and
standing stones.

*Continue driving past the car park to Strumble Head.
Soon the sea will come into view and you will see the
lighthouse. Turn left at the next intersection to park near
the lighthouse or take a walk along the Coast Path (no
facilities).*

**Strumble Head** lighthouse sits on tiny St Michaels Island,
connected to the mainland by a bridge. It was built in 1908
and houses a Fresnel lens illuminated by an electric lantern.
The lantern was once lit by paraffin; the lighthouse wasn't
completely electrified until 1969.

No one lives here—the light was completely automated in
1980. The rocky coastline in this area has long been dangerous
for navigation; in the 1800s, some 60 vessels were lost
nearby.

## Tour 3: St Davids to Porthgain to Fishguard

**Strumble Head lighthouse**

*Return to the main road the way you came in and veer left to follow signs to Fishguard. Soon the Preseli Hills will come into view ahead. At the next junction, turn left to Fishguard.*

*You will pass through a group of houses. Turn left at the small sign for Llanwnda and go about a mile. (You will come back this way.)*

Entering **Llanwnda**, the only settlement on the Strumble Head peninsula, you will soon see a small church on the right at the far end of a large lawn. The church is usually open. It sits alongside the pilgrim road to St Davids and is quite old; in 1881 during a rebuilding project, workers discovered six inscribed stones dating to the seventh to ninth centuries, five of which are set into the exterior church walls today for safekeeping. Walk around the church to spot these, and don't miss the stone with the carved human face.

The church is dedicated to a Breton saint, Gwyndaf, who is said to have been angry at a jumping fish which caused his horse to throw him off when he was crossing a stream nearby. He put a curse on the stream so that it would never again have fish.

About a half-mile walk through the fields behind the church will take you to the Pembrokeshire Coast Path and Carreg Wastad Point, the site of the French 'invasion' of 1797, described later in this tour.

**Church of St Gwyndaf, Llanwnda**

## An Unusual String of Ancient Monuments
The Strumble Head peninsula, or Pen Caer, is full
of Neolithic chambered tombs, Iron Age hill forts,
and field systems. In one especially interesting
find, archeologists have discovered ten small and
similarly constructed chambered monuments
that seem to have been intentionally lined up
across the highland ridge of the peninsula, from
Garn Fawr to Llanwnda to Goodwick.

*From the church, drive back to the next junction and turn
right. At the next junction, veer left toward* **Goodwick**. *To
see three burial chambers, you will need to turn off not
long after you enter Goodwick.*

*At the bottom of a hill as you begin to go through the
village, to the left you will see a steep uphill road, New
Hill Road—it is just across from the Hope and Anchor Inn.
Take that left road to the top and follow the brown signs
to the burial chambers.*

*There is a car park, and the stones are reached through a
wooden gate on the left at the far end of the car park;
there are houses either side.*

The three burial chambers or cromlechs known as **Garn Wen** lie within an area of Goodwick called Harbour Village, which was built to house the workers of the railway and ferry port transportation hub here. In the process, it seems that several other cromlechs were destroyed—the Pembrokeshire Archaeological Survey (1897-1906) reported nine cromlechs here. The area is sporadically maintained, and the cromlechs can be quite overgrown with weeds.

**Garn Wen cromlechs**

*Turn around and go back downhill the way you came in. At the bottom, make a sharp left and then an immediate right turn (not signed) to go down the hill toward the ferry terminal area and into Fishguard.*

**Fishguard** *(Abergwaun)* is best known today as the end of a rail line and a ferry terminal connecting Britain with Rosslare, Ireland. It was once a walled town, founded as a Norse trading post around the year 1000. Its name derives from *fiskigarðr,* a Norse word meaning 'fish catching enclosure'. It has long been a fishing village. After the pirate Black Prince fired cannonballs into the village in 1779, the townspeople built a fort to defend themselves; it overlooks Lower Fishguard.

The Royal Oak pub, in the center of town, was where the French surrendered after their failed invasion attempt in 1797.

**The Royal Oak, Fishguard**

The Fishguard Library, located in the Market Hall across the street from the Royal Oak, houses the impressive Last Invasion Tapestry. Several years ago, 70 local women spent two years hand-embroidering a tapestry depicting the invasion, which they modeled on the Bayeux tapestry that tells the story of the Norman invasion of England. It may be viewed during library hours, and admission is free.

Also in Fishguard and relating to the invasion, you can visit St Mary's Church, on the Market Square, and see a memorial stone honoring Jemima Nicholas, the woman who captured twelve drunk French soldiers as prisoners wielding only her pitchfork. (See the sidebar on the next page for an 1895 account of the incident.)

The Richard Burton and Elizabeth Taylor movie version of 'Under Milkwood' by Dylan Thomas was filmed in Lower Fishguard in 1972, and 'Moby Dick' starring Gregory Peck was filmed here in 1955.

*The tour ends in Fishguard.*

**The Last 'Invasion' of Britain**

The liveliest description of this botched 'invasion' comes from a 1895 book, Nooks and Corners of Pembrokeshire, by H. Thornhill Timmons:

'Usually the most easy-going of Sleepy Hollows, Fishguard town awoke one fine morning towards the close of the last century to find itself become suddenly famous. On February 21, 1797, three French frigates were sighted off the Pembrokeshire coast bearing up towards Fishguard Bay, where they presently came to anchor near Carreg Gwastad Point.

'During the ensuing night the enemy came ashore to the number of about 1,500 men, regular troops and gaol-birds, under the leadership of one Tate, a renegade Irish-American. Tate… established himself at the neighbouring farmhouse of Trehowel, while the main body of the 'invaders' encamped atop of an isolated hill overlooking the village of Llanwnda. Thence the Frenchmen dispersed about the countryside, scaring the inhabitants out of their wits, and rummaging the farmhouses in search of potheen and plunder.

'Meanwhile the authorities bestirred themselves. Under the command of Lord Cawdor, the Fishguard Fencibles and Castle Martin Yeomanry marched out to Goodwick Sands, where the enemy, finding the game was up, laid down their arms and surrendered à discrétion. Thus these doughty regiments achieved the unique distinction of facing a foreign foe on the soil of Britain itself.

'It is said that the good wives of Pembrokeshire, arrayed in their red woollen 'whittles,' countermarched and deployed around a neighbouring hill, thus leading the invaders to suppose that a regiment of gallant redcoats was preparing to oppose their advance'.

# Tour 4

## Fishguard to Newport to St Dogmaels

*This is another rather short tour, about 17 miles, and can be traveled in a few hours. However, if you have the entire day there are several stops along the way that offer scenic walks along the Coast Path. The busy village of Newport is also worth a stop, and just beyond that is the reconstructed Iron Age fort of Castell Henllys. Nevern's church has an ancient Celtic cross, set in a grove of yew trees, and is worth an hour's stop. Last village on the tour is St Dogmaels, above the scenic Teifi estuary, where you can explore ancient abbey ruins.*

>   *From Fishguard, follow the signs to A487 north, toward Cardigan.*

Look far off to right; you will spot the small mountain with the boulders on top—Carn Ingli *(Mynnydd Carningli)*, which means Mount of Angels. As you get closer to Newport, it begins to dominate the view.

A large Iron Age hill fort from around 1000 BC, nearly ten acres in size, sits atop this 400-foot high hill. It was once quite a bustling place, with 25 hut circles, three enclosures, and several walls and embankments. Remnants of a Bronze Age settlement line the lower hillsides. Several walking paths lead to the top.

You will pass by signs pointing to the small village of **Dinas Cross** *(Dinas)*. If time allows, consider detouring into the village and making the circular walk around the Dinas Head portion of the Pembrokeshire Coast Path. It is one of the best short walks on the path, with spectacular views—the highest point of the path is here. It is about 3 miles and takes about 2 hours; there are a few steep parts. One wall of a very old church, St Brynach, sits dramatically by the beach in the hamlet of Cym-yr-Eglyws. The church was destroyed by a terrible storm in 1859, which also caused more than 100 ships to wreck along the Welsh coast.

**Ruins of St Brynach Church, Cwm-yr-Eglyws, Dinas**

*Continue north past Dinas Cross on A487, and in a few minutes you will enter Newport, situated between a wide white sand beach and the slopes of Carn Ingli, on the edge of the Preseli Hills.*

The village of **Newport** (*Trefdraeth*) packs a lot into a small space—the parrog, or wide beach, the Coast Path in both directions, walks up to Carn Ingli, the River Nevern estuary, with birds and other wildlife, a Norman castle (now a private dwelling), a welcoming visitor center, a large car park (turn left on to Long Street from the main road for the last two), pubs and cafes, shops, and places to stay.

Newport began as a planned town in the early 1200s, the main settlement of the Norman lord William FitzMartin. He built an earthen castle here near the estuary. The stone castle you see today at the top of Market Street was built sometime after the mid-1200s. It was partly destroyed during the Welsh uprising in 1408, when Welsh ruler Owain Glyndwr was leading a long and unsuccessful revolt against English rule.

Today the castle is a private residence and not open to the public. The structure lay in ruins for many centuries until it was purchased by a Sir Thomas Lloyd around 1860. He had the large gatehouse restored for use as his home. The Church

**Newport Castle**

of St Mary's, below the castle, probably dates to the 1400s, with renovations made in the 1800s.

> *Leave the centre of Newport and continue on the A487 toward Cardigan. Follow the signs to Newport Beach and golf club at the far end of town. You will see on the right a small brown sign marked 'Burial Chamber' (next to a larger sign for businesses and dental offices), pointing left to a driveway into a group of modern houses.*

A short walk from the road up that driveway will take you to the cromlech **Coetan Carreg Arthur.** This chambered tomb was erected around 3500 BC and not excavated until 1980. Note that only two of the uprights support the capstone. Excavations here have found a few bone and pottery fragments. This cromlech once would have had a commanding view of the sea. Don't confuse it with Coetan Arthur at St Davids Head, which is larger and apparently older.

(For those of you who love to seek out ancient monuments, consider consulting an Ordnance Survey map to locate the nearby and unusual Cerrig y Gof, a circular grouping of five smaller burial chambers from the Bronze Age. From Newport,

**Coetan Carreg Arthur, Newport**

head west in the direction of Fishguard—the way you came in—and drive for a mile or a mile and a half, until you reach a dip in the road. Look for a gate on the right. The stones sit in the field past the gate and can be viewed from there.)

## Castell Henllys

Not along the route of this tour, but just off the A487 past Newport as you head to Cardigan, is a reconstructed Iron Age fort called Castell Henllys. The original fort here was built around 600 BC. Sitting in 30 acres of woodland and meadow, the fort has been undergoing archeological excavation since the 1980s.

Today's re-built structures—four thatch-roofed round houses and a granary—sit on their original foundations. Considered by the experts to be well-done, this is a great place to get a feel for what life was like in the area so long ago.

Castell Henllys is owned and managed by the Pembrokeshire Coast National Park Authority; there are toilets but no cafe. The site is handicap-accessible; contact the park authority for more information (phone 0845 345 7275, ww.pembrokeshirecoast.org.uk).

*From Coetan Carreg Arthur, return to A487 and turn left toward Cardigan. In about two minutes you will see a sign for Pentre Ifan burial chamber on the right. Turn right here to see Wales' largest and most stunning cromlech.*

*Drive less than 2 miles on a narrow lane, following the signs, until you come to a layby where you can park. Then make the short, level walk to the site.*

**Pentre Ifan**, the much-photographed Pembrokeshire treasure, has a capstone (which points to the River Nevern) that is more than 5 meters long and weighs about 16 tonnes. Like all the other cromlechs in Wales, this one was originally covered with earth, which has since eroded or been dug away.

Pentre Ifan, which means 'Ivan's village' in Welsh, dates to about 3,500 BC. Flint flakes and bits of pottery were found during excavations here, but no bones. It is hard to imagine a more stunning site. The high hill you see off in the distance is Carn Ingli. CADW maintains the site, which is open daily, with free admission.

**Pentre Ifan**

*From Pentre Ifan, return to A487 and turn right, then very shortly turn left into Nevern. As you come into the village, go past the inn and cross over the stone bridge. Turn left and drive all the way up to the top of the hill. You will see a small parking area on the right; park here to visit the ruins of Nevern Castle.*

*After exploring the castle grounds, turn around and drive back down the hill. Just before the sharp left turn in the road, look for a lay-by and a stone and concrete ramp on the right. Park here to walk up the ramp and down a path a short distance to see the **Pilgrim's Cross**. The cross is thought to have been carved by pilgrims making their journey to St Davids. A short distance up is the cross, on your right. You will have to look hard to see it, faintly carved into stone.*

*Then continue down the hill into the village to visit the church, to your left at the bottom of the hill. (There is more parking along the road past the church.)*

The ancient and attractive village of **Nevern** (*Nanhyfer*) is well worth a visit. The main attraction is St Brynach's Church, a Norman structure that sits on the site of an earlier religious building that dates to about 550 AD, when Irish settlers lived here. St Brynach, an Irish monk, had a *clas* here, a center of ecclesiastical importance. The impressive tower may go back to Norman times, though the church itself has largely been restored over the centuries. Several lovely old homes and buildings surround the church.

The interior contains two inscribed stones, which have been set into window sills to protect them. The Maglocunus Stone is inscribed in both Latin and in Ogham and dates to the fifth or early sixth century. The Braided Cross, in another window sill, is from the early tenth century.

But the real treasures of this church lie in the yew-tree-shaded churchyard. Look first to the right of the church entrance to see the Vitalianus Stone, which is from the fifth century, is an Ogham stone, inscribed in both Latin 'Vitaliani Emerto' and Ogham 'vitaliani'. These are from the era when the Roman influence was present in the region and Latin was still spoken, when the Irish were living here. Notice the wrongly inscribed 'N'—some think this indicates that the inscriber did not actually know Latin.

This Celtic cross, known as the Nevern Cross and dated 1033-35 on an inscription, is considered one of the finest in Wales, perhaps carved by the same person who made the Carew Cross (see Tour 1). The beautiful panels, carved into dolerite stone on all four sides, are filled with complex patterns, two of which have inscriptions.

**The Nevern Cross**

Even with all of these ancient treasures, most visitors come to Nevern church to see the famous 'bleeding yew,' a tree on the right as you enter the churchyard. The sap from a cut branch has inspired many legends over the years, but the most frequently heard is that a monk was hung from this tree for a crime he did not commit. Before he died, he announced that the tree would bleed forever to proclaim his innocence.

A walk on the path that runs alongside the river will take you up into the woodlands to the earthworks of Nevern Castle, mentioned earlier in this tour. It was built in 1108 and destroyed in 1136, replaced by Newport Castle.

The control of Nevern Castle switched back and forth between the Welsh and the Anglo-Normans for more than one hundred years, an important time in Welsh history. It was built by the Welsh as an earth and timber castle after 1108 and then rebuilt by the Anglo-Normans in the late 1100s in stone, only to be recaptured and later torn down by the Welsh later that same century, to keep the Anglo-Normans from using it again. Archaeologists are still investigating this site. They excavated the castle motte in 2009, and other structures were found a year later. Interpretive signs at the site provide more detail.

*Leaving Nevern, continue past the church on the B4592
toward Moylgrove. In about 5 minutes, turn left toward
Moylgrove, and continue for 2-1/2 miles. Here the road
begins to rise to views of the Irish Sea. At the next T-
junction, turn right at the sign for St Dogmaels to enter
Moylgrove.*

The charming village of **Moylgrove** (*Trewyddel*), set in a little
valley and full of lovely 1800s cottages, is the gateway to
stunning **Ceibwr Bay**. To get there—and be aware that the
lane to the bay is quite narrow in parts—look for the sign
pointing to the left at the bottom of the hill as you begin to
leave the village.

**Ceibwr Bay, near Moylgrove**

Ceibwr Bay is a National Trust property, and there is limited
free parking along the road. The Pembrokeshire Coast Path
runs through this area (no facilities).

*From Ceibwr, take the road up the hill to the left of the
bay. At the T-junction, follow the sign to St Dogmaels.
This will take you back through Moylgrove. Continue on to
St Dogmaels on this road.*

The drive now passes through rolling farm fields and every so often offers wonderful vistas of the Irish Sea. A short distance up this road on the left—hard to see until you pass it—is a viewpoint (with picnic tables) where you can park on a lay-by.

*At the give-way sign at the next T-junction, turn right to St Dogmaels. Soon the Teifi estuary will come into view on the left. Make a sharp hairpin curve to go down into St Dogmaels. Turn right at the bottom of the hill at the sign marked St Dogmaels Abbey, which will be straight ahead.*

**St Dogmaels Abbey**

**St Dogmaels** (*Llandudoch*) is home to the Tironian (Benedictine) Abbey of St Dogmael, which had its beginnings as a priory established by Robert FitzMartin in 1115. There was a Celtic monastery here earlier than that, possibly founded by St Dogfael in the 500s. St Dogmaels was founded as a colony of the Normandy monastery of Tiron, the only one ever established in Wales or England.

## Life at St Dogmaels Abbey

The monks at St Dogmaels began, as one would expect, as a conservative lot, remaining true to their vows of poverty, chastity, and obedience. Most were skilled craftsmen of various arts, as was required by the Tironian order. They also spent much of their time in study and prayer.

After a few hundred years, though, things changed. As the St Dogmaels heritage group Hanes Llandoch explains on its website, quoting a 1992 CADW document, 'In 1402, for instance, at the time of the visitation by the bishop of St David's, there appears to have been considerable deterioration. Due to pestilence and neglect, the number of monks had been reduced to four, but they were consuming food for a much larger number. One of the monks, a certain Howel Lange, had been found drunk and was ordered to desist from drinking wine and meddyglyn (the Welsh form of mead) for a year "on account of his excess and his evil deeds". Evidently, the monks had also been drinking in taverns in St Dogmaels and Cardigan. Moreover, they had been consorting with women, while ordinary people had been allowed to wander in and out of the cloister. The bishop commanded that all these practices be stopped and that none of the monks and lay brothers be allowed outside the monastery without special permission'.

Construction of the abbey began in 1120, and Gerald of Wales stayed here in 1188. The Normans took over less than a century later. It was destroyed during the time of the dissolution, in 1536. The 1850s church on the grounds contains the Ogham stone known as Sarganus.

The Coach House, adjacent to the abbey grounds, is the visitor center for the abbey and is operated by the local heritage group, Hanes Llandoch. It has an interesting museum and displays a collection of early Christian stones, as well as some of the carved stones that once were part of the abbey. It also contains a café and shop, and displays works by local artists. The abbey grounds are maintained by CADW and are open daily year-round, free admission; contact the Coach House for hours and events (phone 01239 615 389, welshabbey.org.uk).

Across the parking area from the abbey is Y Felin, a very old mill, one of the last working stone-ground flour mills in Wales. It dates to at least the 1600s. The current owners have restored the mill over the past 30 years and sell various flour products in their mill shop.

*The tour ends here. Continue following the road into Cardigan (see sidebar) and from there to the A487.*

**Cardigan**

Cardigan (Aberteifi) is in Ceredigion, not Pembrokeshire; the River Teifi forms the border of the two counties. In the 1700s and early 1800s, it was the largest seaport in Wales, with more than 300 ships based here. Today it is a busy shopping and cultural center for this part of West Wales.

The town began when the Norman Robert Montgomery built an earth and timber castle here in 1093 about a mile away from the current castle. The Normans wanted to keep control of the Teifi River and port here. Lord Rhys (Rhys ap Gruffyd, a native Welshman) built the stone castle at its present spot around 1170, after he had taken it from the Normans. But a back and forth struggle continued between the Welsh and the Normans for decades.

Lord Rhys held a celebration of singing, poetry, and music here in 1176, an event considered to be the first Eisteddfod. Cromwell attacked the castle in 1644 and it fell into ruin after that. In the early 1800s the owner tore down several old structures and put up a large house on the grounds. A local authority bought the castle in 2003 and has extensively restored it. When completed, the castle grounds will also feature accommodation, dining, exhibits, gardens, and an education centre.

# Tour 5

# Cilgerran to Rosebush to Haverfordwest

*This tour is about 30 miles long, and you should probably allow the better part of a day. It begins in the ancient village of Cilgerran, south of Cardigan off the A478 in the direction of Narberth. It visits one of the most picturesque castles in Wales, then delves deep into the ancient landscape of the Preseli Hills, visiting a Bronze Age stone circle and other prehistoric sites. The hamlet of Rosebush makes for a good stop for lunch or refreshments.*

*The next stop is the Pembrokeshire County Museum, Scolton Manor. From there, the tour goes to a beautiful little church in Rudbaxton with a most unusual monument inside. The tour ends here, and Haverfordwest, is a short drive south. Travelers may also easily return to Fishguard, Newport, or Cardigan from Rudbaxton.*

Entering Cilgerran, follow the signs to the castle. Parking can be a problem, as there is no car park nearby, but the village is small; park where you can and walk to the castle. It is open year-round (see cadw.wales.gov.uk).

The first 'castle' structure was built in **Cilgerran** more than 900 years ago, in the early 1100s, when the Normans erected an earthworks fortification on the steep cliff above the Teifi River gorge. It was the perfect location for spotting marauding armies and controlling river traffic on the Teifi; the seaport of Cardigan is just three miles away. For a century, the ownership of the spot went back and forth between Normans and Welsh. The stone castle you see today was started in the

1220s by the William Marshal family, the Norman earls of Pembroke.

It was at Cilgerran Castle in the early 1100s, the legend goes, where the beautiful Welsh Princess Nest—daughter of Welsh ruler Rhys ap Twdwr and wife of a Norman, Gerald of Windsor—was kidnapped along with her children by Owain, son of the Welsh prince of Powys. Nest's story is too long and involved to go into here, but suffice it to say that her first lover (probably not by choice), when she was a young teenager, was Henry I, and she had many other liaisons over her lifetime, including two husbands.

Nest's numerous children—perhaps ten— some born when she was in well into her forties, have given rise to the belief that 'half of Wales must have Nest's genes in their blood.' One grandson was the early historian and geographer of Wales, Gerald of Wales, also known as Giraldus Cambrensis; he was born at Manorbier Castle (see Tour 1).

Back to Cilgerran Castle: Like most Pembrokeshire castles, this one was fought over several times during the next few hundred years. It was occupied by the Vaughan family from the 1400s until the early 1600s and then fell into ruins. In the 1700s and 1800s, it became quite a popular tourist destination, and visitors would come up the Teifi gorge by boat to view the romantic ruins high above the river. Well-known artists including J M W Turner came here to paint it. In 1938, the then-owner sold the property to the National Trust, and it was extensively restored.

**Cilgerran Castle**

**St Llawddog Church's Ogham stone**

From about 1200, the village of Cilgerran grew up beyond the castle and has prospered into the present century. St Llawddog Church is medieval and, except for the 1400s tower, was rebuilt in the 1850s. In the churchyard is a Ogham Stone from the fifth or sixth century, inscribed also in Latin: *Trenegussi fili Macutreni hic iascit,* or 'Trenegusses, son of Macutrenus, lies here'. Buried nearby is Sir William Logan, a famous Canadian geologist who mapped the geology of the South Wales coal fields. He retired to this area in 1869, living at the home of his sister, a member of the Gower family, at Castell Malgwyn, up river from here.

> *Walk or drive from the castle to High Street and turn left toward the center of the village, and follow the signs to the river (down the lane next to a food shop).*

At the bottom of Dolbadau Road you will come to a large riverside park (and car park with facilities) along the Teifi. The Coracle Visitor Center tells the story of the village's fishing and stone quarrying past.

**Coracle Visitor Center, Cilgerran**

From the late 1700s and into the 1930s, slate was quarried from along the river banks in several locations, and quarry ruins can still be seen through the woods from the river path. The path to the right (north) side of the car park leads to Llechryd in about a mile and a half.

The ancient fishing boats called coracles—made of calico or canvas wrapped around lath frames made of willow and coated with pitch or tar—were once a common sight here, especially in the days when salmon and sewin fishing were important activities. Today the village hosts coracle races during its annual Festive Week, in late August. (To learn more about coracles, visit the National Coracle Centre in nearby Cenarth, open spring and summer; phone 01239 710980,www.coraclemuseum.co.uk.)

> *Leave Cilgerran the way you came in (in the direction of Cardigan) and return to A478 at Pen-y-Bryn; turn left, toward **Crymych.***

> *You will pass through the villages of Bridell, Rhos-hil and Blaenffos. Continue through the next village, Crymych, and as you begin to leave it, turn right just past the petrol station, at the signs for Mynachlog-ddu and Maenclochog. Shortly the road curves to the left. Continue following the signs for Mynachlog-ddu and Maenclochog. Almost immediately you will see a layby (**not** the place in front of a farm gate, go a little farther) on the left side of the road where you can park.*

---

### The Rebecca Riots

The first confrontation in what became known as the Rebecca Riots took place six miles south of Crymych in the hamlet of Efailwen, along what is now the A478.

Back in 1839, this road was a private turnpike owned by the Whitland Turnpike Trust. The trust, owned by an Englishman, had put up a new toll gate here, and the local farmers—who were already suffering through difficult times—were not happy about it. The toll roads had been built mainly to cart lime (much needed to fertilize the fields) from the coasts to the interior, but many farmers had found ways to avoid paying the tolls. When this particular gate was erected to catch those farmers, it was the last straw.

A group of local men, dressed in women's clothes and their faces blackened, used axes and sledgehammers to destroy the tollgate. Other tollgate attacks followed, and a few months later the Whitland Trust backed off. The protesters became known as the Rebeccas, most probably a reference to Rebecca of the Bible.

Three years later, a new tollgate in St Clears started up the riots again. The Rebeccas once again destroyed it—they simply could not afford to pay the tolls . More attacks followed all over West Wales until local governments carried out reforms a year or two later.

---

Across from the layby is a horse-path sign pointing right. If you walk a few hundred feet up that path, you will come to a sign describing the Battle of Preselau—a spirited and successful campaign after WWII to dissuade the British government from evicting 200 farmers from this historic area to turn it into a military training base. The base was later established at Castlemartin. Many U.S. and British military bases were established throughout Pembrokeshire in preparation for the D-Day landings in 1944.

From this point, if you are a keen walker, you can walk up to the sacred hill called **Foel Drygarn**. This is a hill fort dating from about 1000 BC. On top are three very large and unusual Bronze Age burial cairns. Archaeologists have identified 270 platforms that were once house sites, although not all were occupied at the same time—this fort was evidently used by different groups over many centuries. Iron Age and Roman pottery and other artifacts have been discovered here.

The entire Preseli Hills area, which mostly falls inside the boundaries of the Pembrokeshire Coast National Park, contains dozens of ancient monuments of all sorts and must have been a very busy place 3,000 years ago.

*Return to your car and proceed on this road for about five minutes to the next village, **Mynachlog-ddu**, which means 'black monastic grange' (after the garb worn by the monks of St Dogmaels abbey who would come here); it is pronounced 'min-ach-log-thee.'*

*Pass through the village and take the first right turn, at the sign to Rosebush. After crossing the cattle grid the road veers to the left. This puts you on a narrow road, and you will soon see a large parking area on your left, and standing stones on both sides of the road.*

The stone on the left is not ancient but a recent memorial to Waldo—Waldo Williams, a highly regarded Welsh poet and teacher who died in 1971. Waldo moved from Haverfordwest to Mynachlog-ddu as a boy, when his father was named a local schoolmaster, and his time here is said to have influenced his later writing.

The stone on the right side of the road is a bluestone brought to this spot from the crest of **Carn Menyn** (or **Meini**), the group of craggy outcroppings you see off in the distance. It was placed here in 1989 to commemorate the area where it is believed the spotted dolerite stones at Stonehenge originated. However, British geologists in 2013 claimed that better technology has revealed that those Stonehenge stones came from a hill called Carn Goedog, about a mile away.

**Monument to the Presesli bluestones**

Of course the real mystery remains: No one, even after a few botched attempts to replicate the process in modern times, has ever been able to figure out how the stones could have been moved the 180 miles to the Salisbury plain in the first place.

*Go back to the main road, turn right, and continue toward Maenclochog. In about three-quarters of a mile, just before a modern white bungalow, look on the right for a metal turnstile and a low granite sign marked 'Gors Fawr Stone Circle'. It is easy to miss. There is room to park next to the stile.*

**Gors Fawr** means 'big bog' in Welsh, so be prepared for some fancy footwork. Go through the stile and you will see, to the right about a hundred yards away, a circle of 16 short stones forming a ring of about 72 feet across. About 75 yards past the stone circle, toward a group of farm houses in the distance to the right, are two more impressive standing stones, the tallest about six feet. Some archeologists think these two stones helped the ancient people pinpoint the summer solstice, aligned to Foel Drych, the hill you see off to the right. Others think that these stones might have defined an avenue that led to the circle.

It may not seem like much compared to Stonehenge, but this Bronze Age circle is special because it has probably not changed much for centuries. The Royal Commission on the Ancient and Historical Monuments of Wales calls the site 'a remarkable survivor and one of the best of its kind in Wales'.

**Standing stone near Gors Fawr stone circle**

*Continue on to Maenclochog. Turn right at the next give-way sign. In this area are several standing stones that unfortunately cannot be seen from the road.*

As you enter **Maenclochog**, turn left at the give-way sign and park in the village car park, which has picnic tables and toilets. A sign there describes the castle that once stood here. Excavations carried out in 2007 revealed that a Norman earthworks and timber castle, built sometime after 1093, lies under the car park. There is also evidence of a previous settlement here some 200 years before than that.

St Mary's parish church, first built around 1806 rebuilt in 1880, and recently restored, is on the village green to your right. Inside this church are two fifth- or sixth-century standing stones that came from the Llandeilo Lwydiarth churchyard nearby, one of which has an Ogham inscription. They seem to refer to two members of the same family, perhaps brothers. The standing stone outside the church is a modern placement.

*From the car park, turn right,drive past the church and follow the sign to Fishguard. You will soon pass the turnoff for Rosebush.*

You may want to stop in **Rosebush** for a meal or refreshments at the historic pub, Tafarn Sinc—with walls of corrugated iron and painted red, you can't miss it. It was built in 1876 as the Precelly Hotel. It sits across from the Rosebush railway station, which served the line that shipped slate blocks from the Rosebush quarries in the 1800s to the port at Fishguard.

**Tafarn Sinc, Rosebush**

*Continue on the Fishguard Road, B4313, to the junction with the B4329 at New Inn and turn left toward Haverfordwest.*

*The road passes through the village of Woodstock. In a few miles (just past a sign for Scolton Country Cottages), turn right at the sign to Scolton Manor, the Pembrokeshire County Museum.*

**Scolton Manor** is an 1842 country house built for the Higgon family and sold to Pembrokeshire County Council in 1972. Since then, the interior has been furnished to give visitors a look at Victorian life. The home's original walled garden has been beautifully restored, and a beekeeping centre added; several future projects are being planned.

**Scolton Manor**

# Pembrokeshire Backroads

Scolton Manor is surrounded by 60 acres of park and woodland, with picnic areas and a playground, and is open daily year-round. The tea room is open daily. The country house museum is open from April to October (phone 01437 731328; park phone 01437 731457; www.culture4pembrokeshire.co.uk).

*Leaving Scolton Manor, turn right to to return the main road. In 1.3 miles you will enter Poyston Cross. Veer right at the red postbox to follow that lane. The Haverfordwest Airport will soon appear on the left. The lane will make a sharp right curve; after, turn right at the sign for Rudbaxton. In a few minutes, as you drive down a lovely tree-lined lane, look on the left for St Michael's, the Rudbaxton parish church. Drive through the gate to park.*

**Memorial in St Michael Church, Rudbaxton**

St Michael Church, in **Rudbaxton**, dates to the 1400s and was once called St Madoc's. Inside is an unusual baroque monument of sorts to the Howard family. Five almost life-size figures stand in recesses on a memorial wall on the south aisle. Four of them are holding skulls in their hands. They represent George Howard (on the left, pointing to a skull in his hand), James Howard and his wife, Joanna; and their two children, Thomas and Mary. All but Joanna died in the 1660s— note there is no skull in her hands. She apparently erected this colorful monument in memory of her family. (Open daily from April through September.)

*Leaving the church, continue along the lane until you reach the A40 (it may not be signed but is a major road).*

*The tour ends here.*

*Turn left to go to Haverfordwest (or turn right to go on the A40 to Fishguard, which leads to the A487 to Newport, and Cardigan).*

*NOTE:* If you have time (or are returning to the Fishguard or Cardigan areas) turn right on to the A40 here. The drive up to Scleddau (near Fishguard) is incredibly scenic and offers drivers a panoramic view, on a clear day, of the Preselis. You will also pass through the village of Wolfscastle, which has an interesting past (see the sidebar below).

---

### Wolfscastle (*Casblaidd*)

This village, on the confluence of the Western Cleddau and Anghof Rivers, has two parts; the upper is Wolfscastle proper, and the lower is called Ford. In the upper portion, there is a mound, the remains of a motte and bailey Norman castle from the 1100s.

In the early 1800s, a Welsh historian named Fenton excavating nearby found portions of what he thought was a Roman bath—bricks, pipes, tiles, and painted stucco. Excavations carried out in 2010 revealed only that the archeologists may have been digging in the wrong place.

The belief that the Romans never came this far west in Wales seems to be losing ground, ever since evidence of a Roman road leading from Carmarthen—which was a Roman settlement from about AD 75—toward Haverfordwest and possibly on to St Davids—was discovered several years ago.

---

# Tour 6

## Haverfordwest to Llawhaden to Narberth

*This tour is the shortest, about 13 miles long, beginning in Haverfordwest. It makes a stop at Picton Castle, then continues on to castles in Wiston and Llawhaden. From there it proceeds to the busy market town of Narberth, with its castle ruins, shops, cafes and restaurants, as well its fine museum.*

> *From Haverfordwest, follow the signs to St Clears, A40. Once on the A40, in a few minutes look for the large brown sign on the left for Picton Castle. Turn right here to visit the castle and gardens; otherwise continue to the next set of directions.*

**Picton Castle** was built—or at least the front part of the current building—around 1300 by Sir John Wogan, a member of the Wogan family who owned the Manor of Wiston. It is described as being half fortified manor house and half fully developed medieval castle. Direct descendants of the Wogans, the Philippses, have lived here ever since; they were a powerful and influential Pembrokeshire family in the 1600s and 1700s.

Today the estate is managed by the Picton Castle Trust. If you are there in the spring or summer, you will find 40 acres of woodland gardens to explore. There is a bistro cafe and a gift shop that sells nursery plants.

**Picton Castle**

Picton underwent remodeling and expansion in the 1400s and the 1700s. A Georgian wing was added in the 1790s. Today no one lives in the castle; guided tours are offered at noon, 1 pm and 2 pm; it is a good idea to call ahead to confirm. The gardens are open daily from April through October, 9 am to 5 pm (phone 01437 751369, www.pictoncastle.co.uk).

*From Picton Castle, continue driving east on the A40. After you pass Slebech Retail Park, turn left at the sign for Wiston and Clarbeston Road. After this road turns sharply to the right, take the first left, to Wiston.*

*Turn left at the next junction, continuing to follow the signs to Wiston. You will see a parking area on the left; at the time of this writing, there was a red telephone box there. Park here.*

You are now in front of St Mary Church in the tiny village of **Wiston** (*Castel Gwys*) and directly across the road from the Wiston Castle ruins, sitting high above a cow pasture. This is a well-preserved motte and bailey castle—apparently sitting on top of an Iron Age fort— built in the early 1100s (the remains of the keep probably date to the 1200s) by a Flemish chieftain with the wonderful name of Wizo (which has been translated as Wiston), who also established the church here.

**Wiston Castle**

The Normans at the time were encouraging Flemish people to settle in Wales and help them populate their new conquest and thus subdue the feisty Welsh. The Welsh later tried twice to dislodge the newcomers from this place. Llewellyn the Great managed to finally take back the castle in 1220, which presumably led to its destruction and abandonment; he moved his headquarters to where Picton Castle stands today. This property is privately owned, but visitors are allowed to enter and take a look around, including climbing up into the ruins.

### A Roman Fort in Pembrokeshire

The first confirmed evidence of a Roman fort in Pembrokeshire was uncovered during excavations near Wiston in 2013. Fragments of pottery found at the site likely date the fort's construction to the first century, with later work done in the second century. The Roman road heading west from Carmarthen passes north of Wiston near this site.

Also found near Wiston in the summer of 2013 was a large Iron Age defended farm, on Conkland Hill, one of the largest and most complex ever found in Pembrokeshire.

St Mary Church in Wiston was built in various phases beginning in the 1100s. It was restored in the 1860s. In the churchyard, to the left as you enter the grounds from the car park, stands a monument to some of the soldiers killed at nearby **Colby Moor**.

> *Turn around at Wiston Church and go back through Wiston village the way you came. Turn right at the first T-junction and follow the signs for Llawhaden. Continue to the next T-junction, and turn left at the give-way sign to Llawhaden.*

On the way to **Llawhaden**, you will pass by the fields where the Battle of Colby Moor, a decisive battle of the first English Civil War, took place on August 1, 1645. It was here that the Parliamentarians soundly defeated the Royalists, in a final meeting after three years of war in West Wales.

> *As you enter the village of Llawhaden, look for a car park immediately on the right, next to a modern building that is the village hall. This car park is before you reach the main village intersection.*

Directly behind the hall is the shell of a barrel-vaulted medieval hospice, founded in the late 1200s by Bishop Bek of St David's. The ancient building you see was part of a larger complex of buildings here. Pilgrims on their way to St Davids could rest up here and receive medical care, giving it its name 'The Pilgrim's Rest'.

**Medieval hospice, Llawhaden**

The Bishop's Road ran through Llawhaden, continuing through Wiston on the way to St Davids. In places it follows the route of the Roman road mentioned in the sidebar on page 67.

*From the hospice, continue into the village. Go through the main intersection, following the signs to the castle. A small free car park is directly ahead (no facilities).*

It is a short level walk on a paved lane to the impressive ruins of Llawhaden Castle, maintained by CADW. On entering the castle grounds, the going can be a bit rough at first but becomes fairly level after that. Back in the early 1100s, a Norman bishop built an earth and timber castle here, probably over an ancient hill fort. Later this area was developed by the bishops of St David's as a residence and headquarters of sorts, where the powerful bishops lived and worked.

In 1287, Bishop Bek rebuilt the old castle in stone, and Bishop Houghton continued this work in the 1300s, adding the impressive gatehouse. The structure was used for various church purposes for another 200 years or so and was abandoned sometime in the 1500s.

Almost directly below the castle sits the picturesque and ancient Llawhaden Church of St Aidan (also known as St Madoc), the original part of which was built by the Normans in the 1200s, possibly on the grounds of an earlier Irish 'clas', or Celtic church built by St Aidan of Ferns, a disciple of St David's, in the 500s. A downhill walk will take you there, or you can drive there on the road that turns to the right of the village car park. Return to the car park to continue the tour.

**Llawhaden Castle**

The church is situated next to a pond—but don't fish here without the vicar's permission! The double bell tower dates to 1500. Inside are several interesting animal 'whirligig' stone sculptures and other carvings worth a look.

**A St Aidan 'whirligig'; St Aidan Church**

One story offers an explanation for the ancient stone wheel cross that is set into the outside wall at the east end of the church: '...Aidan, under orders to take a heavy load across the Cleddau, was given a yoke that did not fit the oxen, ye managed to carry the load by finding a new ford across the river at Llawhaden. As this was considered a miracle, a cross was erected there. This legend links Aidan to the crossing point and explains the wheel cross and shaft or early Christian monument  of the 10th century, now built into the east end of the church'. (*Llawhaden Community Association, SPARC pamphlet for Llawhaden.*)

> *From the Llawhaden village car park, return to the village main junction and turn left, following the sign to Haverfordwest and St Clears. Turn right at the junction, then turn left onto A40 toward St Clears. At the Robeston Wathen roundabout, follow the signs to Narberth.*

**Narberth** (*Arberth*) is quite a lively and somewhat upscale market town. It offers many cafes, pubs, and restaurants as well as boutiques, antique shops, and galleries. The Narberth Museum, in its new location off High Street at the south end of town, is well done and contains many interesting stories and artifacts of the town's past. Located on Church Street in the renovated Bonded Stores building, the museum is open Wednesday through Saturday, 10am to 5 pm (phone 01834 860 500, narberthmuseum.co.uk).

**Narberth**

Narberth grew up around its castle, from Norman times, but not much is left of it but ruins. Located at the top of a small hill on the south end of High Street, the castle grounds are open to the public, with informative signs throughout the grounds explain the remaining structures.

**Narberth Castle ruins**

*The tour ends in Narberth.*

If you have time or are continuing south to Tenby, you may want to visit Templeton, described in the sidebar on the next page.

## Templeton

From Narberth, follow signs for A478 to Tenby.
The first village you will enter is Templeton. Part
way through the village, on the left, is a small
park, with panels explaining the area's history. A
map there shows the location of Sentence (or
Sentance) Castle, a walk from here. Not much is
left—just a mound of earth about 15 meters in
diameter. Little is known about this ringworks
fortification, perhaps built in the 1100s.
Margaret's Well, one of the holy wells of Wales,
sits near the castle site.

Some think the town's name may have come
from the Knights Templar, who might have had a
settlement here in the Middle Ages.
The village's layout, with houses lining the main
street each with a garden plot at the rear, is a
good example of medieval 'burgages'.

There are several burial mounds, hill forts,
and standing stones in this general area, but
most are difficult to find or see from the road.
During WWII, the Royal Air Force maintained an
airfield here.

# Index

# Index

Printed in Great Britain
by Amazon